Ants

by Cheryl Coughlan

Consulting Editor: Gail Saunders-Smith, Ph.D.

Consultant: Gary A. Dunn, Director of Education,
Young Entomologists' Society

Pebble Books

an imprint of Capstone Press
Mankato, Minnesota

Pebble Books are published by Capstone Press
151 Good Counsel Drive, P.O. Box 669, Mankato, Minnesota 56002
http://www.capstone-press.com

2 3 4 5 6 07 06 05 04 03 02

Library of Congress Cataloging-in-Publication Data
Coughlan, Cheryl.
    Ants/by Cheryl Coughlan.
    p. cm.—(Insects)
    Includes bibliographical references (p. 23) and index.
    Summary: Simple text and photographs present the color and body
parts of ants.
    ISBN 0-7368-0234-7
    1. Ants—Juvenile literature. [1. Ants.] I. Title. II. Series: Insects
(Mankato, Minn.)
QL568.F7C788   1999
595.79′6—dc21
                                           98-46925
                                             CIP
                                             AC

Note to Parents and Teachers

The Insects series supports national science standards for units on
the diversity and unity of life. The series shows that animals have
features that help them live in different environments. This book
describes and illustrates the parts of ants. The photographs support
early readers in understanding the text. The repetition of words and
phrases helps early readers learn new words. This book also
introduces early readers to subject-specific vocabulary words, which
are defined in the Words to Know section. Early readers may need
assistance to read some words and to use the Table of Contents,
Words to Know, Read More, Internet Sites, and Index/Word List
sections of the book.

Table of Contents

4

Ants can be many colors.

6

Most ants are
black or brown.

Ants have a hard body.

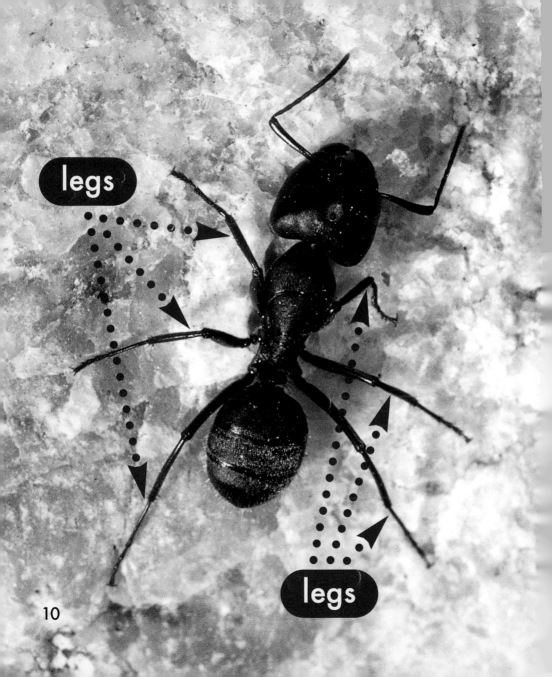

legs

legs

10

Ants have six legs.

Some ants have wings.

Ants have two eyes
made of many lenses.

16

jaws

Ants have strong jaws.

Ants use their jaws
to carry things.

20

Ants live and work
together in colonies.

Words to Know

carry—to hold onto something and take it somewhere; ants can lift objects several times heavier than their bodies.

colony—a group of insects that live and work together; an ant colony can have dozens, hundreds, thousands, or millions of ants.

eye—a body part used for seeing; ants have two large, compound eyes made of many small lenses; ants see movement with compound eyes; most ants also have three small eyes that detect light and dark.

jaw—a mouthpart used to grab things, bite, and chew; ants have outer jaws to carry food, build materials for their nests, and fight enemies; ants have inner jaws to chew.

wing—a movable part of an insect that helps it fly

Read More

Brenner, Barbara. *Thinking about Ants.* Greenvale, N.Y.: Mondo Publishing, 1997.

Demuth, Patricia. *Those Amazing Ants.* New York: Macmillan Publishing, 1994.

Wilsdon, Christina. *National Audubon Society First Field Guide: Insects.* New York: Scholastic, 1998.

Internet Sites

Go to the Ant
http://home.att.net/~B-P.TRUSCIO/STRANGER.htm

Insecta Inspecta World
http://www.insecta-inspecta.com/ants/
argentine/index.html

Teacher's Tower Menu
http://members.aol.com/YESedu/teacmenu.html

Index/Word List

Word Count: 50
Early-Intervention Level: 8

Editorial Credits
Mari C. Schuh, editor; Timothy Halldin, cover designer; Kimberly Danger,
    photo researcher

Photo Credits
Aigrette Photography/Steven Holt, 20
Barrett & MacKay, 1
Bill Beatty, 16
Bill Johnson, 6, 12
Biofotos/C. Andrew Henley, 4
Dwight R. Kuhn, cover, 14
James E. Gerholdt, 8
Rob Curtis, 18
Root Resources/Louise E. Broman, 10